The Life Between

GeoffreyLilburne

The Life Between

West Coast Poems

The Life Between: West Coast Poems
ISBN 978 1 76109 002 8
Copyright © text Geoffrey Lilburne 2020
Cover photo: Sophia Lizares

First published 2020 by
GINNINDERRA PRESS
PO Box 3461 Port Adelaide 5015 Australia
www.ginninderrapress.com.au

Contents

Looking Out to Sea
  Scarborough '83   11
  The Veteran Swimmers   13
  Heart of Oak   14
  Sailboat   15
  Looking Out to Sea   16
  Bingelburra Summers   18
  Dog Beach   20
  Water for Water   21
  Second Life   23

The Lives We Know
  The Lives We Know   27
  The Neighbourhood: Five Years Later   29
  Alan   31
  Playing the Black Keys   33
  Blue Suitcase   35
  Nothing but good   36
  Against Some Resurrection   38
  Procrastination   39
  Like Marmalade   40
  Jessie's Lounge   41
  Beginning the Journey   42
  Prodigal   44
  Next Wash   45
  Time to Pause   46
  Depression   48
  Chemo   49
  Reading a First Diary   50
  Vernacular   51

You May Need Our Help	52
The Near Distance	54
Neighbour	55
Lunch with Graeme	56
Brother	57
My first green ute	58
Going Deeper	59
Loose End	60
Sleep	61
Eleven o'Clock Sunday Morning	62
Farewell Murdoch	63

On the Land

Margaret River, circa 1950	67
Australian Epiphany	68
Seeds	69
On the Land	71
Yard-work	73
Cousin Jim	74
Boab Lament	75
Blue Mountains Uniting Church	76
After the fire	77
Poems not fire	78
The Magic Windmill	79
Adverse Year	81
Chittering Valley Rejoinder	83
Beyond Compare	85
Fury of Destruction	86
Marginal Farm	87
On a wet day at the farm	88
Pilgrim's Rest	89
Fool's Gold	90

After Harvest	91
Summer Hay	92
Sufficiency	95
Autumnal	96
Disciple of Solitude	97
Three Score Years and Ten	98

We are not a sea people by way of being great mariners, but more a coastal people, content on the edge of things...
Nowhere else on the continent is the sense of being trapped between sea and desert so strong as in Western Australia.
There are roos on the beach and shells out on the plain.
Tim Winton, *Land's Edge*

Looking Out to Sea

Scarborough '83

It's my first morning back;
we breakfast on fruit salad
coffee and scones, then walk
by the ocean. Smooth, turquoise-green
waves breaking far from shore
the sky blue, defying thought.

We pass the hotel which stands
hunched against the wind's attack
like a sentinel. My father remembers
his honeymoon in '42 –
two days leave
shortened by love, by sun.

In '21 he came here as a child
the beach deserted
nearly drowning in a pothole.
I ask if this is the site
of the infamous 'Snakepit'
where tides of sin and rock and roll,
first broached these shores in '55 or 6.
It's all here, like some paradise,
lost, regained.

The sun bleaches everything,
retaining nothing.
Native sons do sit-ups on the sand
or ride the surf on tiny twin-skegged boards.
There's a skin on the surface
we dare not break,
yet the light in my father's eyes
tells me it is not forgotten,
his smile makes it real
as if for the first time.

The Veteran Swimmers

Before I'm done, they start to arrive;
white-suited attendants with muted
voices and eyes that look away,
a man with one leg wasted,
another with scar tissue
from shoulder to breastplate.

In locker rooms, they light
cigarettes, strip with single arms,
or just sit. Their grunts and nods
whisper of padded hospice spaces.
At pool-side, empty wheelchairs,
tell all they've taken the waters

that will not heal. High above them
the ceiling arches, restraining
the cold touch of heaven. A fine mist
rains upon the steady splashing
of their several strokes and stripes.
In water, each is born again.

Heart of Oak

Trapped inside I tread these boards
and wish my legs were bowed
on some bucking deck
I guided to distant shores.

Oaken heartwood floors
polished to high gloss
creak underfoot, sustain a sense
of sea, ancient sheeted vessels.

Moving from room to room
I gaze out of portholes
now west down a sloped valley
now east at my neighbour's lot.

Rustle of rain on rooftops
muffled noises map a world
outside, cast mine in high
relief – quiet, dry, protected.

I am the ship
lights probing deeper
I journey to a space of silences
uncharted and immense.

Sailboat

I'm missing an old wooden boat
so fine on the inland lakes of Ohio.
She sails into my dreams like an ancient hulk
wooden stringers still define her shape
pulling me back to a life I knew
across the deep distant seas.

Somehow I want to reconnect
repair the damage of the years
restore, get her sailing again,
I visit the old club, musty rooms
boats half buried under silt
She must be here somewhere.

Or was she made of fibreglass
and moulded sea-green
and did I sell her to an eager sailor
who still plies these waters
weekend by weekend.
as in golden days before?

Where is she now?
Each time I come
a little closer to beauty of her
line, the thrill of her lift
in the breezes of a long-gone era.
I'll sail her someday soon.

Looking Out to Sea

That whole year faced to the sea.
Wet winter afternoons found
treasures beneath the waves
tropical reefs in *National Geographics*,
The Coral Island. I knew
shipwreck and resurrection,
civilisation refashioned from
the bits and pieces that float ashore:
such Aboriginal freedom
should soon be mine.

I saved pennies, cool drink bottles
bus fares, slowly building
towards the magic figure –
five-pounds-twelve, next summer
my first rubber surfboard.
Yet that year's wisdom declined
to spend five-pounds-twelve
on a piece of moulded rubber,
sank into a safe deposit
never to rise again.

Now at great expense
we summer by the sea.
The children's surfboards
come in styrofoam, moulded
plastic and fibreglass.
Theirs is the Coral Island.
Still I look out to sea.
Standing among southern breakers
I see sailing vessels describing
voyages I will never make.

Bingelburra Summers

for Lynley

On the day of the last regatta
I see an old, brick-red Chevrolet
loving snub with flared nostrils,
truck bed clear, shorter than I remember

sleeping there a time or two with you.
Dick and Mark have sailed and won.
Where's your boat? they cry,
autumn sunlight glinting like memories,

coaxing me to back to when
we lived with you in the old mud brick
house and mornings were digging
for mica in the brown cow paddock,

or floating a home-made canoe in
the creeks' drying waterholes.
I tell them, not today, not tomorrow,
no more this year or next. The farm

is sold and the old truck scrapped,
there'll be no more Bingelburra summers.
As the northern winter draws in
we put the boats away for the season.

Soon the lake will freeze, the club
vacantly host a few remaining hulks.
Then I'll be gone, and spring sailing
will start without me.

This year I'll go south and
summer might find me with you
leaning towards some amusement,
a bush picnic, a midnight feast.

Dog Beach

Some run but most amble
gaze at ships far out at sea
trail yellow or green pouches.
Let off leashes, they are careful
to observe their boundaries.
The dogs know no such constraints
gambol in the sand, pounce on waves
sniff passing trade.

Along the strand
thunder thighs coax lean, hairy legs
footprints mingle, pockmarked paws
a line of submerged fallen arches.
As sun sinks into the waves
the long homeward trek
is lightened for every walker
by this communion of beasts.

Water for Water

Your hands were red and chapped
hauling heavy towels and sheets
from the slippery boiling water
of the chip burning copper one
blustery day. A red check scarf
framed the youthful line of your skull,
with rabbit's ears sprouting up
like twin exclamation points.
Back then you did it all for him
and me, with few elements to aid you,
a roughened broom handle, water
and a child with your own bright eyes.

Thirty-five years later
I catch you on the dock. 'Hold Mum'
and the boat's painter moors you
in place as I take out the camera,
focus and shoot. Once again, your hair
is up with rabbit's ears
and I am surprised to see
how you invade your youth
as if by accident – my oversized
sailing duds on you, casually
exchanged for your travel clothes.
In the boat now, fresh winds stir
the sails set and you move into place
like a cat at home with sea,
the fearful heeling of the deck.
Your weight seems light as you move
back and forth, and we're making way
a balanced team, a perfect craft.

In spite of your protests,
'no clothes to wear', 'leaving
Dad behind', I have you now
in a lost pocket of your life.
Deny it if you will, keep it
out of sight if you can,
I'll not relent.

You gave up on water
though water was your element,
the river down Hawksburn Road,
the wide Swan where you swam
and sailed those sunlit days of
childhood. How could you know
that one day a boy would look
at you and laugh, deride your legs
as too fat for the beach,
that taking his words you
would forsake the water as
you had forsaken your youth?
So tell me, if you let him
take it then, mustn't you now
allow that he give it back?
I want to return the gift,
eye to eye, water for water,

Second Life

My Christmases have come and gone.
What's left
        to look forward to?

New Year's Eve upon the sea shore
waves roll in and ripples spread
        over the darkening ocean.

I think of my next destination.

Will it be like flying out to sea,
skimming across the water
becoming one
        with all this immensity and depth,

not a thing to fear
an encounter with totality
        beyond thought or hope?

Maybe I'm wrong about death,
but for now I stand upon
        this sandy beach
                in wonder.

The Lives We Know

The Lives We Know

It was a short street bounded
at one end by the Highway
and the other by the River –
places of risk for the urchin
I was on Hawksburn Road.

Here I glimpsed my first boat,
(a sublime shape that moved me
beyond words before words)
collected nasturtium seeds for Mummy.
I ate chili, once only,
drove my first green wooden ute,
played with Granny, sculpting groceries,
romped with cousins and most of all
felt safe in Daddy's arms.

He took me to the end
of the bus line. I watched him
clear a soldier block of huge jarrah,
banksia and zamia with hand-tools,
axe, sledge and spade.
I slept in a special boy's bower
made of gum leaves and branches
in the shade of a broad tree.
At night we took two buse
back to the distant street.

Hawksburn Road is no more,
swallowed up by urban development
and the Burswood Interchange,
but almost every day
small boats are departing
from the foot of disused streets.
Children marvel at the line
of craft carrying them from here
into the lives they know.

The Neighbourhood: Five Years Later

The dream houses have shrunk,
that strikes you as odd.
You try approaching at twilight.

Here's Tom's; front porch garlanded
with brightly coloured lights.
You'd think it was a brothel
if it wasn't Christmas time.
The interior of the house is lit
with shadows, no one moves.
She moved out some years back,
you're not welcome any more.

Todd and Leann?
Moved away with Atomic Energy.
The house we worked on
that fine summer
has taken a step back
though in the twilight it still bears
the marks of our work: front porch
skylight, cedar walls and red trim.
Settled now, back in line.

Mark's still in business, truck parked out front.
Here's Frank's house. VW convertible,
you can tell he was an architectural dreamer
just by looking. We shared
the summer but he saw only two more.

The attic of Patty and Lew's lit up like it never was.
You can see the frame supporting the roof.
The cars are foreign, new to the block
though nobody notices but you.

Other houses too;
Dennis's seems like it's falling down.
His wife and kids have left now:
he's still working on his doctorate
and teaching part-time.

Houses remain. Like lives
we renovate them for a while
and then let them settle.

We think they will bear us
straight to heaven, but they don't.
They root us deeper in the earth.

Alan

We get off the school bus and walk back
a block before crossing Cambridge
lugging our bags down Boulevard.
You are ahead of me, you were always
faster, blue eyes flashing, blond hair
curled back with lick and style.

You moved easy on the football field
breaking away from the pack
gained possession of the ball
dropped it to your boot
and kicked a goal.
A born player
you took possession of your life
ran with it. Like an adult
you spoke to my mum
and I heard the words that made me
tremble: love, sex, woman.
You caressed and knew them
before you had a right to know
yet landed on your feet
even when cruelly knocked.

I see you now on that football field
fluid limbs tanned skin
beauty in your eyes;
the Paul Newman look, still there
under hooded lids and hair all gone grey.

How then could I comprehend
your sudden, careless end;
how you fell from a speeding car
broke your neck, done at nineteen?
Lips trembling, I spoke
to your mother and father.
Alan, Alan, third son,
beloved one.
'Well, at least he lived,'
her voice faltered, not wishing
or needing to say more.

Now twenty years later
my tears press me.
Why has it taken so long?
All I know is that you're here:
I am amazed how patiently
you wait for me
as we cross Cambridge
angle our way home along Boulevard.

Playing the Black Keys

To the child he hadn't kept faith,
afraid to camp in Pemberton's icy valley
and easily forgetting the promised
cruise to the rugged north-west

despite the boy's longing for an adventure
with his dad. If only wishing
could make it so, imagining on every visit
the hospital corridor a ship's passage.

The farm he dreamed they'd work together
in the nearby hills that could not be afforded
though the lad did good costings and
never told the sadness not to burden

the man who lived at wit's end,
keeping just ahead of the Depression
he knew would return one day,
ill affording ease, a hope not his to give.

But there was music in the evenings
the harmonies of banjo mandolin
the felt-lined carrying case hand-
crafted for the child's descant recorder.

Together they played 'Pedro the Fisherman'
'Jesu' Joy of Man's Desiring.' Winter
mornings he lay in bed soaring with my
piano scales, my flying arpeggios.

When there is nothing else, I remember
how he sat whole nights at the keyboard
swaying out his chords and intensities
playing on the black keys, more easy to reach.

Blue Suitcase

An old blue suitcase
bears my father's name
in simple block letters
handwritten with care
for whoever might inquire
who was the quiet man
carrying it round the world

to me. The distance points
like an accusation
until it seems that
each solitary thing
I've chosen: career,
religion, each relocation
has driven me farther

from him. The blue case
lies on my dishevelled bed.
I touch it,
run my fingers down
the upright letters,
the name they trace
and can no longer forbear
the pressure in my eyes
or the ministry of tears.

Nothing but good

An odd saying of my mother's
I will place upon his lips.
As the fading light of day
blurs edges, endings
night visions dance.

Hi Dad, it's me!
Hello. Can't talk now.

But Dad I need you
to help me with this.
Not now. I can't…

Hey Dad, it's me.
I can't help now.

Dad, I've built a wooden dock
for the boat. I don't think
you've seen it.
I can't come.

But Dad, I just want
to show you.
Dad…?

As the connection fails
I remember the farm years
packing a bag for the day:
food; a change of clothes;
my box of tools for fencing,
framing, straining,
returning in the dark,
dreaming of the perfect farm.

Just him and me,
an adolescent fantasy come true.
Now he's gone, it seems
the best thing I ever did.
Together we made it, he faded
from my daytime life,
but at night…

Hey Dad, it's me.
I can't talk now.

Dad, you remember…
No memory, son.

But Dad, I remember.
Yes, lad, you remember.
It is good. There's
nothing but good.

Against Some Resurrection

Coming up from the plane
as one from the dead,
face cracked open with
embarrassment and gladness,
you stiffened against my embrace,
shook hands instead.
Walking with your bags
the long empty corridors,
you kept bumping into me.

I did not complain
knowing that we live
by approximations,
like Julia
puzzling her race
and saying she was grey.
I wanted to tell her
we exaggerate in each case
when we say white or black
and the union is richer
livelier than grey.

Still I note
how you called me 'Lud'
and once said 'Thanks, love'
instead of 'Thanks, Lud.'
How silently I stood,
grey approximation of a man,
how all these near misses stand
hollowing out the heart
against some resurrection.

Procrastination

My father stays out back
won't come into the house
to face his death. He doesn't
draw attention to himself,
prefers to pass by unnoticed.

He finds a well to dig
a wall to build. He uses
old tools that need mending.
I knew his jig was up when I saw
his claw hammer missing a claw
and drill bits he'd inexpertly
sharpened. He wouldn't come
to his funeral, so we had to proceed
without him, which was awkward.

Someday soon he'll
have to come in, face the music,
Till then we humour him with
little chores, paint the eaves, Dad,
clear the gutters, mow the lawn.
But obviously it can't go on like this.

Like Marmalade

Darkly mysterious, the jar
on the pantry shelf foments
its mouldy secrets
in back space silence.

As a matter of course,
he visits the old lady, interrupts
the vacant spaces of her day.
Startled, she looks up –

unable to complete
a single sentence. A silence
hangs between them until
she says his name.

Like marmalade
on the tongue, the taste
as fresh today as when
she bottled long ago.

Jessie's Lounge

The pink rose by the settee
in Jessie's lounge reminds me
of the time my mother posed
in pink knitted cardigan

and white half-gloves
at this very same place;
she loved 'ye olde worlde'
of the Metropole.

When lucidity failed
she asked for nothing,
fearing only the nonentity
she would become.

We sat at her bedside,
shocked at the finality
of her departure pose.
Too late for words then.

Now, I sit here with all
I wished I'd said, but didn't.
Beside me, the pink rose
blooming in summer sun.

Beginning the Journey

There was once a buff-coloured Ford
Prefect fresh from Uncle's showrooms.
Dad knew how to drive it, so in we hopped
Bev and I in the back, Mum in front.

Now there was no limit to our range.
We drove to the farm at Chittering,
down to Albany for Easter, or out to
Mundaring to see the weir overflow.

But Dad progressed to Holdens as
his rank in the company rose;
white and gold, then green,
all with cigarette lighters and shiny grills

Mum drove the little Prefect
and we bounced along through
lessons, let off the clutch gently
Joan, kids roaring in the back.

Next was my turn, by this time
the old Ford was green and I
rebuilt the engine and drove
her all over the dating scene.

My first loving occurred in these
padded seats and soon she took
me off to my first job, junior master
at Applecross Senior High.

Then one day she faltered
with a flat battery and I was sold
on a wrecked VW from Uncle's
used car yard, coloured grey.

Dad drove the Prefect into
the underground garage
parked her, locked the door
and threw away the keys.

One day I'll find those keys,
locate the old Prefect,
and drive her away.
Mum and Dad in the back now.

I can't wait for that hour
to hear those four cylinders
ticking over, laughter in the air,
our journey just beginning.

Prodigal

Silence fogs windows
this sodden Sunday.
Unable to sail my Comet
I scream, family is
forced confinement.

When I see the open fields
with downed corn stalks
and a foot-worn pathway,
I wrench the car door open
stumble outside.
I search the ploughed ground
for some hint of grace,
find only old corn husks
like rats drowned in a flood.
It strikes me
I am disappointed
with this kind of death
just when a light breeze
moves clouds above my head.

Without a key I knock.
My daughter opens
her quick smile
lets me in.
A meal is set,
my plate is full.

Next Wash

I pick your hairs, one by one,
from my cream and black striped shirt.
I pull them off, cast them away
as if now, finally, I am shed of you.

These few stray hairs – all that
remains of our compromising passion –
I remove relentlessly, religiously,
absolving us of all implication.

And they will be gone
and we will be done
and all will be well.

But the hairs are soft brown;
there's a slight crinkle to them.
I cast them off more gently,
pausing to remember your touch,
the persuasion of your embrace.

And they will be gone
and we will be done.
My shirt will be clean
in the next wash.

Time to Pause

Dammit! Everything is broken!
Always in a hurry
deadlines to meet
cows to be milked
a paper delivered or
emailed to the editor.

You need time
when everything is broken
to mend it piece by piece
separate each single fault
pare each severed thread
and make it right again.

Sequence is everything
nothing quite what it seems
when everything is broken.
You open the first fuse
but it might blow again unless
you fix the pressure pump.

A false step spells disaster
in the chain of repairs
black dog usually on heat
when everything is broken.
The earnest Mr Fixit
must look outside himself.

Only one recourse now,
you sit in a dark room
and chant Eastern prayers.
It fixes nothing, but at least
with everything broken
it won't upset the karma

The universe sighs as you
ponder the folly of human
invention and intervention.
Time to be still and wait:
supplication makes sense
when everything is broken.

Depression

It comes like the dew overnight.
Next morning
everything you touch
is covered.

Phases of the moon move blood.
Ocean tides creep
into hidden estuaries,
familiar marshlands.
Quietly, insidiously
seepage enters me.

I wake to fear
some sudden
unbidden
descent.

Chemo

This time last year I was on chemo
chemo sucks the life out of your blood
blood red scarf I tie around my head
head for the hills, avoid the clinging crowd
crowd around a single defining thought
thought I'd live to a hundred
hundred chances I've missed this time
this time last year I was on chemo.

Reading a First Diary

The boy, beginning to be man,
offers all his doubts and fears
to the scrutiny of an absolute
all-seeing introspection
which he confuses with God.

He finds little space for freedom,
for comfort, is continually needing
to check that his way is proper.
Older friends collude, keeping him
in bondage, as he struggles
with new energies and possibilities.

He moves toward the discovery
of what love is, whom he
will love, will become.
Go, young lad,
before your heart breaks
break free,   break free.

Vernacular

No worries, mate, she's apples
someone says, Thank you,
so we say it. What we mean
is, Sure, you're welcome,
not at all, I'm just being polite here.
It's a habit we get into
and there's another one too,
the anxiety habit. Most live
forever fearful that something
might go wrong. What shall we
worry about now, now that the mortgage
is paid off, the alimony squared away?
Perhaps it's the kids, a dip in super
income, there'll always be something.
An engaging, death-dealing habit.
No worries. What if we meant it,
what if there was nothing
to worry about, ever? Sure
you might face a life threat
then caution, care are needed
extreme caution, extra care
but not anxiety. *No worries, mate*.
Oh my God, what if it really
were true. It would be something
like God is love. *Bugger me!*

You May Need Our Help

Yellowed with age and dusty
from its long sojourn inside
the Bakelite 1940s wireless
a card falls to the bench
MORRIS RADIO SERVICE.

Back before
instant global communication
phones rang and small lorries
roamed empty streets
for no home could be without
its mantle radio set.
DAY OR NIGHT
FOR PROMPT ATTENTION RING
BA 5540 (Perth) UA 1833 (Mt Lawley)
OUR SERVICE VAN WILL CALL.

Valves lit up and rubber perished
on sheathed wire
but 6IX, 6PR or posh 6WN
offered essential lifelines
connection with the world
beyond the picket fence.
Morris Radio Service offered
REPAIRS TO ALL RADIOS.

These days it's all transistors
you don't wait for faults
just buy the newer model – junk
the old. No cards will be discovered
in heaps of e-trash.

Treasuring this find
I rehearse the careful moves
of long departed Morris men
fondly coaxing this vintage
back into life.
PLACE THIS CARD IN YOUR RADIO
YOU MAY NEED OUR HELP

The Near Distance

She wants only the lightest touch
moist lips pursed for the kiss

she will place upon my cheek.
I want to give more, to insure

the long day ahead, food,
protection from its dangers…

already she is moving toward
the door, telling me it's okay

today she's buying lunch, cash
in hand. I leave dishes, follow

to the step, her friends waiting
a block away, No need to hurry,

be careful crossing the street
I want to say, but it's so quiet,

I remember myself, draw back
to my minor role. The orange

bus is flashing there, drawing
her on and all I can do is watch

my child cross streets and
move off into the near distance.

Neighbour

Shrunken into retirement, no more
patents pending, plans to see the world
he mows grass with an old red mower
or slowly trims the back hedge
looking up with genuine shock
when you greet him – though
for years you live next door.

As days turn colder
trees start to shed
he gathers leaves by hand
placing each crinkled shape
in his yellow plastic bucket
as if they were the days of a life
and not one should be lost.

Lunch with Graeme

Back when I was 19, you were 21
my big brother, you owned a car
I rode an old Lambretta.
You knew your way in the world
I wasn't at all sure. What energy we had
for our women, our hockey, our surfing,
the deferred exams in Anthropology
that summer we shared at Kingswood.

Now, in late autumn, we sit in sun-light
a couple of old fellows, moving into shade.
More comfortable, we lick our wounds
reminisce about our early marriages
past wives and our present reality.
You put new batteries into your
hearing aids while I keep mine
turned up to catch every word.
God still rates for both of us

(we hope we still rate with God)

We talk of what we do in the church
how we struggle to keep up with
our grown kids, grandchildren.
It's been a long journey, mate.
We have weathered the storm
and every squall is worth this kind
of remembering, this kind
of attention.

Brother

I had just placed my cap
upon the vacant chair
when he said: I hope you don't mind
if I keep mine on while we eat.

Usually I laugh at his silly old lids
so I just grinned in amusement.
When he took it off
looked me in the eye

I saw sorrow in his face
his thinning hair, receding hairline
features aged well beyond
his mere three-score years.

I do not enjoy seeing a kid
brother humiliated like this–
some genetic accident.
In future I keep my hat on.

My first green ute

made of wood, before
plastic and Matchbox
beyond our reach.
Dad's hand with old tools
wheels spun on tiny axles
steered by a wire lever.
No Brumby, Hilux
four-wheel drive this
loaded with opportunity
for small boy confined
to city streets, concrete slabs
grey lines, before the open
fields of farming, green grass,
spreading trees, tractors
seed drills. I drove that
green ute everywhere
with love – up sandy hills
down muddy creeks,
a geography of possibilities
untold, still mine.

Going Deeper

Riches await the one who sits
by a sunny window, warm cup
in hand, pen and paper at his side
he will end his day as he began it.

There is work to be done
he is not ill or lacking strength
but all he will achieve today is
to mend fences, straighten bent posts.

He may summon words or he may not
it is enough to savour the moment
he has seen many things, many places
but coming home finds something else

a pool hidden in Chittering hillside
is a loch by stormy Scottish seas.
Growing deeper in silence
its profound stillness
calls forth speech.

Loose End

He was at a bit of a
loose end. He'd had
the golden handshake.

Still food on the table,
pension cheques in the mail.
Is this how it ends? he asked.

The whimper announcing
one final handshake to go?
Nah, new horizons, they said,

it gets better, you'll see
Just don't come unstuck.
Well, I'm stuck, all right.

What's to look forward to?
No new start-ups, promotions
in the pipeline. Look, forget

beginnings and changes,
it's all cyclical!
So it's a bike, is it?

Pedal treadlemill
with backpedal brakes
no longer needed?

Sleep

My love affair with sleep
has me bedding all over town.
It's getting me into trouble.

Friends say I'm sleeping
around, tell me it's time
I woke up to myself.

Afternoons find me nipping out
of coffee breaks to make for
the couch, napping time I say.

This passionate desire
for sweet oblivion might spell
trouble before the final lights out.

As I see it, I'm just snoozing
my way through meetings
I'd rather not attend.

Eleven o'Clock Sunday Morning

Hour when the godly are in church
and the ungodly still in their beds

and, stranger to both camps
I track the pavements and verges

taste the hints of early spring
in the thawed ground, warm

beneath the sharp wind
feel my body light on its toes

brisk in movement, brace
to face the wind, answering

spring's incipient warmth
with an unbidden surge of hope

and feel pulsing through
this body-soul a promise

kept for godly and ungodly
touching even Sunday stragglers.

Farewell Murdoch

I wandered onto the old campus
with some overdue books for return;

parking permit expired, offices
empty, bookshop moved.

Perhaps a coffee for old time's sake,
catch up with mates from before.

The University Club demolished
no friendly tables, this wandering

begins to feel aimless. Reluctant
to sever any remaining contact,

I clutch the books more tightly.
Perhaps the life of the mind

will again call and I will take up
further studies in brain chemistry

or the treatment of depression.
And perhaps I won't. Instead recall

nine happy years, and simply say
farewell Murdoch, farewell.

On the Land

Margaret River, circa 1950

A wide-eyed town kid
early in the frosty cold –
draws number houses in white chalk
on the shed's cement floor.

Lumbering cows file through
the bails, their breath making clouds
in the still morning air.

Frothy whiteness flows
into giant cans. Auntie mixes
sweet coffee essence with hot cream
for the family of workers at fireside.

A milky smell like comfort
fills this lonely shed in the corner
of a vast, wintry continent.

Australian Epiphany

Uncle Bob's been firefighting again this year. He comes from smoking bush and threatened livestock to this family celebration, eyes strained as he passes his genial greeting from one to another. After the shared meal – ham, chicken, vegetables, rolls, nuts and steaming hot Christmas pudding topped with sticky yellow custard and whipped cream – he will go with my father and other uncles to lie in the cooling shade of the old banksia tree on the back lawn. There they'll exchange stories. Bob is a spinner of tall tales of the bush, always a twinkle in his eye, even when teasing his sophisticated, city-bred nephew.

As the day's heat reaches its peak and long before the sea breeze brings relief, they will fall silent, start to snore. I will try once more to ride the new bicycle, will fail again, setting scratches like sins which multiply and remain on the once-shiny mudguards. But the breeze will come as it always has. Bob, Dad and the others will wake for games, more stories, tea, cake and ale, our living room regaled with scores of coloured cards depicting jolly little snow scenes or shepherds on an open hill, lights in a purple fractured sky. Then, Dad at the piano, 'Joy to the World', 'When Irish Eyes Are Smiling', our laughter and reminiscing flow into the night.

At the end they all go away. I am left with my chipped bicycle, my leather-bound Bible and Handel's *Messiah*. I wonder if God goes out with them to the fires, the smoking stumps and fences, or if God dwells in my house, its sudden silence and emptiness. I listen for rustling of the summer's breeze, find comfort in the warm darkness.

Seeds

1

I was thirteen, as I remember,
when my father's elder brother
took me to work with him.
He was careless, oblivious of my sins
as I strained at my manhood
and felt released.
Gasoline bit my nostrils
with the sharpness of energies
long stored, and I worked
the tractor's brute strength,
stiff clutch and high steering wheel.
And seed, not sticky, but dry
with dusty phosphate
was drilled into virgin soil
(not spilled or wasted)
fashioned rough windrowed acres
into farmland pasture.

2

In southern suburban streets
you see seeds drifting
from an unseen Cottonwood;
they glide to earth
trailing white plumes behind,
gather in gutters,
by kerbsides; messes of foam.
We sweep them up without a thought,
throw them out like trash
or scraps of memory that conceal a gift.

3

Driving through country fields
this early spring day
I see the corn stalks ploughed under,
the brown loam turned upon itself
waiting to receive any gift
the earth or sky might bring.
Did I see this then, or only now,
that there are no unholy energies
and that all our seeds are scattered
with an abandon like a god's,
as if there was always more
and nothing would ever be lost.

On the Land

If you want to know

where a man is a man
and a boy is a man in waiting
you can't go past, the man on the land.

His feet are planted
on solid ground
so much else is false and shifting.

The man on the land
does his yeoman duty
when others fall aside.

Hands are broad, brow furrowed
but on his back he bears a tribe
feeding and clothing us all,

or so I thought as a lad.
Don't be ridiculous! Dad said.
All I wanted was to be a farmer.

A career later
I bought a small hillside block
and worked it with my hands.

Every year I lost money
and now I say
to the man on the land

Get big or get out
the small farmer is a
threatened species, a dream past.

Refusing the agribusiness myth
I farm with love and for love.
Amply rewarded

the man on the land
is his own master, no man's fool,
lifeblood of a people.

Yard-work

It was good of you to come
at last in late afternoon.
The work started badly
mower wouldn't fire, died
two times before a wheel
came loose, bellying the cutter
in the grass, a round scorch mark,
loneliness in the middle
of a wide green day.

I worked on the broken mount
and it came more easily,
one job calling forth another.
I pulled the frayed cord
and contact! You were there
as I swept the path,
clearing away mown grass,
walnut shells, dry leaves.

I keep thinking of you,
never happy without a job and
once at it, going like a demon,
pausing for neither breath
nor contemplation until
you've worked a complete
transformation.

Cousin Jim

(In memoriam, Spencer James Lilburne)

You always reached for the thrilling edge, sailed
ocean-going yachts and caught errant fishers,
crashed and bashed around your outback place,
those few hundred acres of scrub and bush

where just last year I paid a visit;
drove up to Mullewa and slept in the shed
housing your caravan, which recalled Grandad Jim
who lived out his days in a tent in a shed in Moora.

We gathered fresh sandalwood in the old ute.
Like me, your 'twin', you hankered for
the pioneer life, guns and shed in the bush,
helped me with seeding on my few acres.

'Spencer the garbage man', the boys called you,
your habit to pick up cast-offs from others
make something useful out of metal or wood
in your shed with tools and lathe.

The cancer claimed you with its dreaded grip.
Let it not have the final word – I will remember
trips far out to sea, straining sail, buffeting
winds, and the fragrance of cut sandalwood.

Boab Lament

This Kimberley's a hard place.
I grow thick porous skin, distend
like a pregnant mammoth
to store the water of life.

Last night a boy dropped
from my branch
like an unripe plum.
Why is it always the boys?

Is it a Kimberley disease?
At his funeral they will sing
a brown man hung on a tree
whom Earth could not hold.

But here I've seen too much
sickness, blight, and death.
Is there no root or leaf,
no Worowa song to sing this whole?

Blue Mountains Uniting Church

First thing you notice is the sign.
The bird has flown, no blood remains
in its spread wings. The Reverend
has been taped over, blank and nameless.
'Everyone is Welcome' somehow
fails to convince. Don't expect
a crowd to flock at 9 a.m. for
the nameless, faceless; or rush
to dial a number in faded digits.

The stained glass is still intact
and the tower has been restored –
reminders of a neglected faith
a citadel of what once was.
A sharp red arrow points to the rear,
Lifeline shop open for business
promises a bargain or two –
a sign of life, the eternal variety
no longer on offer.

After the fire

Driving west, at last reaching that final
bend in the road, I see the posts are
gone and the gate flattened –
ring-lock and barb a tangled mess.

All before me is ashen
pasture, tree trunks black,
fallen where they burned,
now blocking the drive.

Car abandoned, I continue on foot.
Fences all down and the cattle yards
– so carefully build with old Bert –
just charred shards. Sharp debris

crunches underfoot, staining my shoes
black beyond hope. But then, I see it
on the far hill – iron roof shimmering.
A benediction in morning sunlight.

Poems not fire

Four steel stumps set in concrete –
all that remains of our sturdy workbench.
Termites consumed the soft wood surface
where we never engraved our names.

Fire ripped through the cattleyards
in a single hour. That marvellous fencing,
wires strained with the old ute,
posts cut from dead trunks, all gone.

You too passed through flames
no flesh survives.
If I return to the scene
of our wondrous adventure,

will you whisper to me
as in our day
of poems not fire, not age
can take away?

The Magic Windmill

A lever is pulled. The Yellow Tail
swings into line behind the big fan.

Gathering speed, rods push and pull
fresh water out of dry ground.

I watch it swing this way and that
lifting from the depths an old story:

a wooden crate from windswept Chicago
making its way to the dusty railway siding

at Perenjori on the Midland line.
A boy sits wide-eyed as Pop

plays with his giant Meccano set.
And look! The pieces fit together.

Excitedly the old man joins strut to cog
frame to stand, and soon an entire Aermotor

is turning smoothly in the hot dust.
All that remains is to put it up.

Sixty years later, my aged father
dreams of a new Aermotor cranking

on the Chittering farm we work together
OK, Dad, let's do it. You make the calls,

I'll foot the bills. Months pass,
a year, nothing happens. To his dying day

he dreamt of this magic windmill.
Wouldn't it be lovely is all he would say.

I sit for hours – the Yellow Tail
spinning its potent spell, a spring

rises up. No longer alone
I'm seeing Perenjori through his eyes.

Adverse Year

i

I did not find her, little black cow
though I immediately noted her absence
from the small herd, dejected in dry summer paddocks.
I stomped over hill and rock with my stumpy knee
and found neither carcass nor spoor of this one.
Rang the neighbour, you got a visitor in your herd?
No news is bad news, but I do not give up hope
that my little black cow will return to the fold.

Another lot arrived looking lean, and the seller told
me in passing that a bull might have visited
one or two. Nothing came, or so I thought,
until one day she was missing. As I paced
the stumbled acres, I saw a white mound,
Oh bloat, I conjectured, until I saw the calf's
head, just born before mother fell to rise no more.
Now both are gone, a mound of carrion for passing
crows. The calf's head, like the mother's, was white.

ii

This gal would not go in gates, waited till the very last
to move up into the forcing yard. Biggest and most
beautiful of the herd, she'd grown accustomed,
dare I say, fond, of this hillside pasture.
Sharing her sympathy, I felt a tug of something
nameless, as I tried in vain to hurry her.
Finally, at the end of the race she refused
to leave the good earth for the truck bed,
all 425 kilos resisting the last spring
into her gallant future, a nameless place
in the food chain.

Nervous Nelly, brought only a dollar and five
for her glorious kilos, and I wondered at the value
of sending her on a journey from a place she adhered to
for rough yards, a blood-slick floor, the meat hooks.
Cattle men have no hearts, but as prices fall
another currency seems to arise.
I think I will eat more vegetables
in the coming year.

Chittering Valley Rejoinder

> …take grain from the header
> from the whale's stomach as Jonah watches on…
> 'Chaser Bins', John Kinsella, *Jam Tree Gully*

In my wellies and Drizabone
I stumble out of the drizzle
to the sheltering veranda.
Hungry animals chomp on the lines
of dry green feed I articulate
in their very presence – absence
of words bothers them not a whit
but I reach for the laptop
and the whole task comes to this:
what to say to John Kinsella.

I too would wish for plain sailing
sheltering like Jonah in the belly
of this giant called productive
farming – soil, plant, animal finding
a way to live and not reduce one to
the other in harmful monoculture.
Choose the no-production mode
if you must, but allow for some
to strive for another culture
whether perma… or multi…

Your whale or mine might spew
us out upon the beach if we
persist in too fierce a retreat
from reality. Nineveh calls,
let your university job keep
hands warm and soft
for penning verses.
Mine grow cold and hard
publishing lines of hay
for mouths to feed us all.

Beyond Compare

Well, I've got forty-five horses under the hood
a throaty diesel, starts like a charm
every time, and when I climb up
it is my throne, the lord of this valley.

You might say, a lesser machine
would have done well enough here,
these few acres and a meagre half living.
In six years, only two hundred hours.

Let me tell you – the old grey Ferguson
was not enough, mechanical brakes,
a danger on hilly slopes, no way
for old men with metallic knees.

Now here's my big red tractor, bulging tyres,
front end loader, three point linkage,
hydraulic lifting at my fingertip,
power brakes, four-wheel drive. Oh boy!

You may snicker, you godless Prius prickers –
I will enjoy this diesel extravagance
the rest of my days, be born aloft
with heavy bales into realms of grace.

Fury of Destruction

Row upon row of upright wheatstalks
each bearing its gift of ripening grain
just over the hill and down the slope
starts the salt, now in white and pink
with only saltbush to survive the scald.

Dead trunks gesticulate toward the sky
as if to protest the violence done to this
once gently wooded landscape – for man
must come and clear the trees for crops
and with the felling of the last tree cover
salt slowly rises and land is poisoned.

Dead now for a thousand years, a seeping curse
turning our sweeping landscapes into desert.
Salt is spreading, land is dying before our eyes
still more fertilizer is pumped onto the surface
to produce another crop for this year's harvest,
preparing the way for the bitter return of years
to come. Driving through this country, we marvel
at the ingenuity of man, a fury of destruction.

Marginal Farm

'What saves it is to love the farming'
Wendell Berry, *The Making of a Marginal Farm* (1980)

Rocky slopes, tree-lined
some steep, some gentle
fall away to a few acres
of rich, loamy soil.

My views are stunning
out across valley floors
and peaks. Gazing out
I take stock.

See margins spent
on summer feed
to sustain a small herd
breed another season.

Husbandry here
with eroded pastures
few acres to till
profits little,

Unless the seed
and harvest are one;
a higher love
for a hillside farm.

On a wet day at the farm

Maybe it's my age
or perhaps the weather
but I can't help looking around
and saying, All this, so much of it
is magnificent. How does it come
to be here, whose hand made it?
There's a house, there's an orchard,
shed, hay fields, cattle yards.
Evidence of many hands.

When first we came there was nothing and
we had little, Dad and I, our bare hands,
an empty tin can, some rudimentary tools
from his backyard. What we had was dreams,
visions, hope, energy. So we worked, day after day,
not noticing that whenever we did, something
changed, something grew and remained. Now we
have all the remainders of those days, the tailings of
that labour, and like the Lord Almighty, on this wet day
I say, it is good, very good.
Blessed be.

Pilgrim's Rest

How it prospers
this little farm of mine,
house quite snug
with insulated ceilings
and green-painted trim.

A small herd munches
dry summer grasses
The shed full of hay,
baled on a few acres
at foot of the hill.

An old ute transports
me around to inspect
dam and tank levels,
animals' progress.
It's a pilgrim journey.

In this place there is no
Slough of Despond
only green and distant
vistas to please eye,
succour spirit.

Fool's Gold

All day it was building
>storm clouds gather
>>barometer falls.

It waits till we sleep
>before the drip, drip
>>turns to roar

Of water falling
>running off dry ground
>>gushing from gutter spouts.

Ah, life in the desert, we say,
>green feed for stock
>>refreshing the fields.

But wait! Soon it dries, dicots die,
>pastures depleted.
>>Disillusion.

After Harvest

Of course you love the ploughing
summer feeding of hungry beasts
but the best feeling all year
come rain or shine is crop secure
shed full of baled hay
you swing the door shut to bar
inquisitive cattle and stray kangaroos.

This year, a new shed packed
to the rafters with aromatic hay
grown on our few arable acres –
no matter it's weed-infested
hungry cattle will gladly munch
in lean, dry months ahead.
For a week or so, as days lengthen
and temperatures soar, you rest
with this thought – harvest home.

Summer Hay

The work I love, the season least adored.
Push the shift into high ratio in searing summer heat
parched air moves over hands and face in the open cab

Open the gate, bales in serried ranks.
Select the nearest, skewer it with front-end loader
soon on its way to waiting black Angus cows.

Dolly comes trotting, in front of the load in her eagerness
to tongue the fresh wheaten hay. Binding cut,
whole sheaves fall off, the rush of hungry beasts.

I watch them, gladdened this year to have
such luscious forage on this dry, comfortless day;
riches to share with this herd of noisy munching

music to my ears. Oh grow sleek, little ones,
give us calves to fatten for next year.
Let it happen. This farmer's yearly prayer.

More Land

He lays a hand upon my arm
Looks me square in the eye
Mate, we want to sell our land
We'd like to offer it to you.

I take the old wagon and drive
the rutted track up the Galloway block,
longer and deeper than mine,
and then the all-year dam at the back.
Such beautiful land, madness
to let it slip through my fingers.

I do my sums – if I sell this
and cash in my super perhaps
I could just afford it.
By running 20 steers I could make
2 grand a year… Is it enough?
Almost, a real stretch without reserves.

Some folk come to us as friends
but we must drive them off.
Jesus said, Get behind me Satan
to his closest disciple, Peter.

Haltingly I say my noes
and the circus begins without me
an agent engaged, signs go up.
The chance slips away, my fingers itch
take up an old volume of Schumacher
bloody small is bloody beautiful.

Small is Beautiful: Economics as if People Mattered, E.F. Schumacher

Sufficiency

It is enough
this hillside farm
my dog to run free
cattle grow fat.

First thing
crank up the old ute
a tour of inspection.
Overnight nothing has moved
cows munch on hay
fires die down, grass damp
with early morning dew.

Naturally
I could want more
but if the Lord is shepherd
leading into green pastures
by still waters
I shall not want.

Autumnal

How rapidly the green fades
as year advances past its prime
growth ceases and the process of
dying begins, with glorious coloration
the ripening of seed crops.
I watch the fruit trees deepen
their shade, begin to put forth
buds of new fruit for the year.
It's a time to sit and consider
consolidate the increments of
spring nearly over. I move towards
my end, gather what trophies I may
massage losses and aches
number my days and apply my heart
to wisdom. It is very good, now, to
rest in shade for a quiet season.
This golden spring time feels
like a treasured autumn.

Disciple of Solitude

No doubt he loved his fellow man
but what he preferred was this,

gentle discipline of solitude,
waking to the quiet space of hills,

still green trees, a distant
cawing of crows. A songbird in its

hidden nest, he comes home,
food on the table, labour of hands,

silence to let the day emerge as it will,
as it will, as it surely will.

Three Score Years and Ten

I drive down the winding gravel track to the bottom double gate, braking to swing open the way into the hay paddock. The steel pickets lie in a mess of tangled barbed wire which pricks my skin and brings up a bubble of blood on my scarred hand. It is no matter, the blood will dry and the wound will heal, for this is Australia and I am at home. Contentment comes knocking as I pound the post into place, the sledge hammer loose on the desiccated handle, so that I have to pound it back with a rock picked from the pile at roadside. A centimetre at a time, the steel picket moves into the sun-dried loam and stands. Soon I can stretch the wire taut, and make something of a cattle-proof fence against the depredations of beasts seeking water from the well head. I won't deny them water, but prefer they drink from the nearby trough which is full and leave the pump head to carry out its job. This is my place, a bore I've sited and sunk, a mill I've put up, and all works together as it should, if things can be restrained and kept from breaking out. Once I wanted to change everything, usher in a just order of peace and brotherhood. Now I will be happy if the cattle will leave the bore head and the windmill turn in the late sea breeze and the land know a cooling trend, and I will live at peace with all things.

www.ingramcontent.com/pod-product-compliance
Lightning Source LLC
Chambersburg PA
CBHW070048120526
44589CB00034B/1598